Methodism in Walsingham
in the 19th Century.

John Hawkes

Published by R. C. National Shrine, Walsingham

First published in 1998 by the R. C. National Shrine,
Pilgrim Bureau, Friday Market,
Walsingham, Norfolk, NR22 6EG.

ISBN 0 9502167 4 7

Printed by
The Lanceni Press Ltd, Fakenham, Norfolk

A Walsingham Centenary Publication

1.   Walsingham 100 Years of Pilgrimage 1897 - 1997
   (R. C. National Shrine, 1997)

2.   Walsingham England's Nazareth by Peter Rollings
   (R. C. National Shrine, 1998)

3.   Walsingham Methodism in the 19th Century by John Hawkes
   (R. C. National Shrine, 1998)

Front Cover Illustration used by kind permission of Rev. John Denny.
Photograph: The Pulpit of Little Walsingham Methodist Church during the
Ecumenical Festival of Flowers for the Centenary of R.C. Pilgrimage.

FOREWORD

The contents of this book are written as a tribute to the Methodists of Walsingham, past and present. Part of the text was a special study for the Open University.

I have lived in Walsingham for nearly eighteen years and have been privileged as a Catholic deacon to be included regularly on the "Plan" of the local Methodist Circuit. In this I have followed in the steps of Fr. John Murphy, sm, and Fr. Gerard Langley, whose spirit of ecumenism led them to assist in leading worship in local Methodist Churches.

Fr. Alan Williams, Director of the Catholic Shrine invited me to allow the Shrine to publish this little book as an ecumenical gesture in this Centenary year of the restoration of the Shrine.

Local Methodists including the Chairman of the District, the Rev. Malcolm Braddy, M.A., who has written a greeting at the beginning of the book, have entered fully into the celebration, forging yet another link in ecumenical relations.

John Hawkes

Little Walsingham Methodist Church

INTRODUCTION

In my study there is a photograph of a smiling Roman catholic cleric, John Hawkes (see previous page). He is surrounded by Methodist dignitaries along with the custodians of the Roman Catholic and Church of England Shrines in Walsingham. We were all together to celebrate the Bicentenary of Walsingham Methodist Church in June 1994. The photograph shows how warm our ecumenical co-operation is in Walsingham, and all the Methodists know that John is a friend of the whole Circuit as well as the local church. We also know that he and others in Walsingham take ecumenical risks, although these remain within the boundaries of respect for all our traditions and our people. With this background, John is admirably suited to write about the development of Methodism in the 19th century.

You will find here a well-documented account, showing the strengths and weaknesses of the Methodist system. The prophetic fervour of the early Trades Union leaders and the strong standards of morality are both things from the past which we need today.

During this period of Methodist development we kept alive the religious fervour, devotion and desire for Christian perfection which is exemplified in the pilgrim people who used to come to Walsingham and, since the 30s, have returned to Walsingham. It was our privilege to maintain a pattern of piety which was suppressed by bigotry for several centuries.

Methodism has, of course, continued beyond the studies outlined here and we hope that this reminder of ministry and mission in the 19th century will prove the bedrock for our continuing ecumenical ministry in the 20th century in Walsingham through the grace of God.

Malcolm Braddy
Chairman of the District
Trinity 1998

Contents

Page

Chapter One

Walsingham, Old and New
in the 19th Century

Kelly's Directory of 1845 described Little (New) Walsingham as a "neat Market town of 1155 inhabitants situated in the valley of the river Stiffkey. There is a small market on Fridays and a fair on the second Monday after Whit Monday. The greater part of the land is owned by the Lord of the Manor, the Rev. D. H. Lee-Warner and also that of Great (Old) Walsingham."

The fame of the place began in about 1061 when a Chapel was built here in honour of the Virgin Mary and became a great centre of pilgrimage throughout the Middle Ages. The change came when Henry VIII, a former pilgrim to Walsingham, ordered his officers to destroy the Shrine taking away all that was valuable.

Ruins of this great shrine still exist and are included in plantations and grounds of the mansion of the Lord of the Manor, open to the public. The parish church of St. Mary's is large and contains many beautiful features, having been restored after a fire in 1961.

The Directory noted that there is a Wesleyan Chapel built in 1794 and also an Independent Chapel, The Shire Hall, Bridewell, a House of Correction, a Workhouse for the Walsingham Union at Great Snoring. There was a free Grammar School and a National School, Alms Houses and several generous charities.

There were generous provision of medical care, veterinary surgeon, shops to supply the needs of villagers, seven Inns and taverns and several tenant farmers. Coaches and Carriers commenced with London, Norwich and Wells on several days of the week. There was also a Post Office. Great (or Old) Walsingham contained 426 inhabitants with two inns and nine farms. The ancient parish church of St. Peter was in joint living with Little Walsingham. "Obviously residents look to Little Walsingham for services, trade facilities and transport."

Chapter Two

The Coming and the establishing of Methodism in Walsingham.

(a) Wesleyan Methodism

We know that John Wesley came to New (Little) Walsingham in 1781, where a Methodist Society had been formed in 1779. His visit is recorded in his Journal on Tuesday 30th October 1781. He wrote -
"At two in the afternoon, I preached at Walsingham, a place famous for many generations. Afterwards I walked over what is left of the famous Abbey, the east end of which is still standing. We then went to the Friary; the cloisters and Chapel whereof are most entire. Had there been a grain of virtue or public spirit in Henry the Eighth, these noble buildings need not have run to ruin."

Although some minute books for the Society at Little Walsingham are not available, the Account Books of the Trustees from 1793 can be examined. This was the year when the building of the Chapel began.

One of the earliest entries states that "The building of Walsingham Wesleyan Chapel was begun 10th June, 1793." We read that the first foundation stone was laid at the south west corner by Mr. William Westdrill, Officer of Excise, the second at the north west

William Westdrill, Officer of Excise, the second at the north west corner by W. Minns, Miller, the third at the south east corner by Martha Lambert and the fourth was laid at the north east corner by Mr. Denton the assistant preacher. Regretfully there are no signs of these stones today.

The Chapel was built almost certainly within the sight and probably on the foundations of the 14th century Franciscan Friary. The present ruins of the Friary cover 2½ acres, but originally that property covered 13 acres, which means that for over 200 years, Methodist worship has been taking place on a site which first witnessed Christian worship over 600 years ago. The Manse garden covers the high altar area of the Friary Church, beneath which is a crypt, yet to be excavated. On a dry summer day, the footings of the pillars of the great church can be seen alongside the two cloisters and the domestic areas of the Friary. (See Plan of Friary in Appendices).

The Manse, garden and schoolroom are now owned by the Knights of Malta and are used for the care of sick and handicapped pilgrims. From time to time, the adjoining Methodist Chapel is used for their services.

The Account Book records "The church was opened by worship on Sunday 8th June 1794 by Mr. Charles Boon, the preacher at Yarmouth and Chairman of the District. The text taken was Hagai Chap 2 vv 7, 8, 9."

"And I will shake all nations and the desire of all nations shall come, and I will fill this house with glory, saith the Lord of Hosts. The silver is mine and the gold is mine, saith the Lord of Hosts. The glory of the latter house shall be greater than of the former, saith the Lord of Hosts, and in this place will I give peace, saith the

Be it Remembred that on this Ninth Day of June in the Year of our Lord 1794 it was Certified into the Registry Office of the Lord Bishop of Norwich by a Certificate under the Hand of William Denton of the parish of New Walsingham in the County of Norfolk and Diocese of Norwich bearing date the Third day of the same Instant June, That a certain now erected Building called a Chapel situated in the parish of New Walsingham aforesaid, is designed and set apart as a place of Religious worship for Protestant Dissenters according to an Act of Parliament in that case made and provided Witness my Hand —

Rich. Moss
Depy Regr.

Certificate authorising Religious Worship

The details of the expenditure and subscriptions are given as follows:

"Building and furniture   about £750
Specified items include:-
a time piece   £6 - 13s - 6d
Carpenters work   £215 - 92 - 6d
Bricklayers work   £115 - 6s - 6d
Beer to the carriers of bricks and tiles   £1 - 12s - 6d."

The Chapel House or Manse cost £105-10s-9d and its furniture cost £48-1s-6d. The resident minister lived in the Manse for some time, but moves around the circuit by Ministers was quite usual, e.g. there was a ministers house at Docking.

"In 1876, the Chapel House occupied by the resident minister for around eleven years was being rented by the circuit stewards at £10 per annum - but they were £31-10s in arrears." Kelly's Directory for 1845 records that the Wesleyan Minister Rev. J. W. Cotton, lived in the High Street.

This Church is the oldest Methodist Church still in use in East Anglia. It is a typical chapel building of the period, four-square brick with arched windows and pillared portico. The tiled pyramid roof is topped by a weather vane. It certainly meets the instruction of the Methodist Conference Minutes of 1790, which stated "All preaching houses in the future are to be built on the same plans as the London or Bath Chapels." referring to Wesley's Chapel, City Road, London.

In 1846 considerable damage by fire is recorded. The Chapel accounts of 1849 note "Bill for repair of damage caused by fire breaking out in Mr. Coker's premises and communicating to gig-house and cottage July 1846 - £10-9s-9d." Kelly's Directory of 1845 records a Mr. J. Coker, gentleman, living in the High Street.

Fortunately, the original box pews of the church were preserved, but Victorian restorers of 1880 replaced the pews on the ground floor.

The accounts entry states:-
"May 19th 1888. Paid 2 men for removing old pews to Mr. Woodcock's brewery 3s-0d."

Of the pews, there is no indication of the reason for removal of those on the ground floor, but those of the box pew design are still preserved in the gallery.

Original Box Pews

The pulpit (shown on the front cover) was also replaced for it goes on later to state, "March 2nd 1890 received from Mr. Back for old pulpit 5s - 0d."
N.B. Mr. Woodcock was a butcher living in the High Street and Mr. Back was a brewer trailer and draper of Knight's Street (Kelly's Directory 1879.)

The schoolroom was built on the site of the Manse stable in 1890 at a cost of £229-15s-11½d. It is indicated that most of the expenditure on renovation and building was met by public subscription which shows that at the end of the 19th century the Wesleyan Methodist cause enjoyed strong support in the village. The building work of the schoolroom was carried out by Charles Tuthill, Builders and Contractors of Wells Road, Fakenham, the payments which were made in three instalments are shown on receipt in the circuit records at Fakenham.

We read, however, that another loan was needed, this time from Mr. George Wright a prominent Methodist from Great Walsingham. £60 was borrowed and gradually paid off, supplemented by a grant of £7 from the General Chapel Fund, the national body in 1895. Mr. George Wright is recorded in Kelly's Directory for 1900 as a "Miller (steam roller and wind) baker and farmer." He was obviously a man of substance and typical of those who were the local leaders of 19th century Wesleyan Methodism.

(b) Primitive Methodism

In 1811, Primitive Methodism came into being from largely a reaction against formalities and rigidity which had developed in Wesleyan Methodism and from the famous Mow Cop Camp meeting, in which William Clowes and Hugh Bourne took part, after which, the final breakaway of Primitive Methodism, took place.

It was very much a new revivalist movement which spread to Norfolk and by 1825, circuits were based in Fakenham and Norwich. There followed a rapid expansion of Primitive Methodism in East Anglia with an increase of six circuits in 1825 to 19 circuits in 1842, thus we find the Primitive Methodist Chapel built in Walsingham in 1848 in an area that had come to be known as the Martyrs Way, the route believed to have been taken at the Dissolution of the Priory by two Walsingham martyrs, Thomas Guisborough and Nicholas Mileham to their place of execution above the village, now known as the Martyrs Field.

The building of the Chapel demonstrates the divisions in Methodism which had taken place in Walsingham since the death of Wesley. The building still stands and is typical of the traditional preaching house of the period. It was sold in 1933 after the 1932 Methodist Union, in which all major Methodist traditions came together.

The purchaser of the building was Mr. Faircloth, of a well known Methodist family, who converted it into two houses for his workers in the family butcher's shop. The only item of internal furniture remaining is the pipe organ, now in the Wesleyan Church in Little Walsingham. Some interesting stained glass windows can be seen at the rear of the building, alongside some attractive ceiling covings in the upstairs interior. Two commemorative plates of the Centenary of "Mow Cop" 1807-1907 now hang on the pulpit in the 1794 church which probably originated from the Primitive Methodist building.

Chapter Three

Religious Census 1851

The only official Religious Census ever taken in Britain was in 1851 which showed that 4.4% of the English adult population were Methodists. It gave details of the dates of buildings, including houses given the Certificate which permitted worship.

In Walsingham, four places of Methodist worship were recorded in which, as well as indicating the numbers of sittings available, gave details of attendance at worship on Sunday 30th March 1851 as follows:-

1. <u>Wesleyan Methodists</u>
   Chapel erected before 1800 (i.e. 1794)
   The spaces available were: 220 free sittings.
                                220 other sittings.
   Attendance was as follows-
                                17   Sunday School
   General congregation   116   Afternoon
                                70   Evening
   Signed Daniel Hateley, Minister.

2. Wesleyan - Walsingham Union
High Street
The General Congregation was-
64   Afternoon
60   Evening
Signed Joseph Curzon, Manager, Grocer and Draper.
(Joseph Curzon was a prominent Wesleyan Methodist).

This Walsingham Union as it was called in the 1851 Census was probably a gathered congregation of dissident Walsingham Methodists under the leadership of Joseph Curzon who signed the Census form and may have met in the Union Workhouse off the High Street in which there was a meeting room.

The Norfolk News of 12th January 1851, the year of the Religious Census, reported a meeting "held at the Independent Chapel on 7th January to express sympathy with expelled Wesleyan ministers and condemnation of the tyranous proceeding of the late Conference".

About 300 were present. The Chair was taken by W. H. Agnew Hardy. In his speech, he analysed the law of 1835 and made it clear to the common-sense of all present that it is a law".
"Shaped in" apostacy and unbelief (RF) he goes on to claim that "it was a duty to agitate." (RF)

The formal split among Wesleyan Methodists began in 1849 resulting in an expansion of Methodist places of Worship. In Walsingham, the breakaway group did not obtain a building for Worship until 1868 when the group bought the Independent (Congregational) Chapel. It is interesting to note that the original meeting of dissent took place in this Chapel as we read in the report of 12th January 1851.

The Wesleyan Reform group was particularly strong in Norfolk but bitterness inevitably accompanies the split of 1851 resulting in difficulty of obtaining suitable premises for worship. Bitterness inevitably accompanied the split; difficulty in obtaining suitable accommodation may have exacerbated the bad feelings. It is interesting to note that in 1868 the Congregational/Independent Chapel now part of the Anglican Shrine complex was sold to the Free Methodists and they continued to use it until the end of the 19th century.

At the middle of the 19th century, up to 100,00 lay people left the original Wesleyan body and in 1857 these "breakaway" groups formed together to form the United Methodists Free Church as a separate body. By 1972 they had 10 circuits in Norfolk and Suffolk with over 2,500 members.

3. Wesleyan Methodists - Old Walsingham
    Not a separate building, but believed to be at "Hill House", still a private dwelling.
    Spaces available   150 free.
                              180 others.
    (This indicates a cottage church with out buildings/barns).

    Attendance   30 Morning.

    Signed Robert Goodman,
    Local Preacher, Great Walsingham.
    (Kelly's Directory 1854 records Robert Goodman as a gardener).
    There was a preaching house certificate issued for Old Walsingham in 1792.

4. Primitive Methodists
    Built in 1848 (Martyrs Way).
    Spaces available   50 free sittings
                                 176 other sittings

    Attendance   73 Sunday school
    General Congregation 172   Afternoon
                                 172   Evening.

    Signed William Werel,
    Primitive Methodist Minister.

It has been claimed by some church historians that the figures in the 1851 census were not accurate and that their authenticity was determined by the clergy and others who completed the returns.

Chapter Four

Chapel Life and Activities

(a) Trades Unions

Of the contribution of Walsingham Methodists to the social and spiritual life of the village and district, that of the pioneers of trade unionism for agricultural workers must be counted among the greatest. The Primitive Methodists of Walsingham led by many of their Local Preachers established the roots of agricultural trade unionism as Nigel Scotland writes -
"In all these struggles, Methodist theology played a unique part. The doctrine of Christian Perfection was an incentive both to good works and self improvement."

Methodist belief in spiritual equality provided the roots for social equality. We read that on Wednesday 12th November 1873 the

Walsingham District of the Agricultural Union established by Joseph Arch held a public meeting in the Walsingham Primitive Methodist Chapel. The verse of hymn they sang on this occasion summed up their aspirations -
"All people now assembled here in union raise a cheerful voice.
Not all the world shall make man fear,
Who in a righteous cause rejoice." (Tune "Old Hundredth")

Scotland in assessing the influence of Methodism in promoting action by the labouring poor of the countryside writes -
"The building and establishing of a Chapel was often an act of open rebellion against parson, squire and farmers."

Thus we find in almost every village the building of a chapel and the establishing of a Methodist Society. These chapels gave a dignity and purpose to the farm labourer who by the second half of the 19th century were without rights to the land and human dignity. They had come to be regarded as ignorant and backward and were thus mocked and became the subject for satire. L. Marion Springall writing in 1936 of "Labouring Life in Norfolk Villages 1834 - 1914" referring to the place of the labourer -
"At the Chapel he could conduct a meeting, even if he were illiterate, provided he had the dignity of character, an understanding of his fellow labourers' needs and some capacity for public speaking." Much of the strength of Primitive Methodism was in its democratic system!

No better example of this labourer could be that of Zacharias Walker, Walsingham District Secretary of the National Agricultural Labourers' Union. He was the Primitive Methodist Circuit Steward, Local preacher and Trustee and Sunday School superintendent.

His preaching duties regularly brought him to Walsingham which was part of the Fakenham Primitive Methodist Circuit.

Another local preacher, frequently in Walsingham, was George Edwards 1851-1933. In his autobiography, Edwards wrote -
"God alone knows and we know how my parents worked and wept, and the sufferings and privation they had to endure ... I have seen both faint through over-work and lack of proper food."

An old people's home in Wells-next-the-Sea "Arch House" is a memorial to Joseph Arch 1828 - 1919, trade union Leader, Primitive Methodist Local Preacher, who rose from a crow scarer to be the Member of Parliament for North West Norfolk. His grace before meals is telling -
"O Heavenly Father, bless us,
And keep us all alive,
There are ten of us to dinner,
And food for only five."

In the words of Joseph Arch, the farm labourers were "underfed, overworked, uneducated, voiceless, voteless and hopeless."

Nineteenth Century Methodism in Walsingham, as in the rest of the country, established Sunday schools wherever Methodists ministered. At the end of the century, the Wesleyan Methodist Conference reported that over a million children were being instructed in the connexional Sunday Schools. George Edwards, born in 1851, wrote, "This was the only schooling I ever had."

He records that when his name first appeared on the circuit plan in 1872, he only knew the letters of the alphabet! It must be emphasised, however, that in spite of union and political duties, the religious commitments of these men never suffered. Edwards writes, "On Sunday I attended my religious work for I never neglected that for anything."

Many Victorian farm labourers showed a great independence of spirit in that they were prepared to refuse charities dispensed by the local vicar as Scotland writes, "They were ready to reject the parson's coals and his wife's blankets and to organise their own benefit and sickness societies ."

The agricultural workers union took many of their structures from Methodism. They held Union Camp Meetings often followed in the evenings by a Union Love Feast. This gave structure and solidarity to union organisation. In many villages, Primitive Methodist Chapels were used for meetings and the word "Chapel" was used to name some unions. It is still in use in some print unions today.

Wesleyan Chapel - Chapel/Manse/Schoolroom

Many social advantages followed the establishing of unions and we read that Frances Sands, Primitive Methodist, local preacher and a member of the Walsingham District Union established a co-operative store at Docking in 1875. A further social benefit was the establishing of Union Sick Benefit structures in which money was provided at times of sickness. Scotland records, "One of the first Sick Benefit structures to be founded was at the Burnham Branch of the Walsingham District." Assistance was, however, two ways and we find that the Trustees of the South Creake Lodge of Odd Fellows gave a mortgage of £130 to the Primitive Methodist Chapel at New Walsingham on 29th March 1880. The Receipt is shown below.

d.
1 per Sheet.

18015

1880. March. 29th

We the undersigned Trustees of the South Creake, Lodge of Odd Fellows do hereby acknowledge that we have his day received of and from the Trustees of the Society at New Walsingham called the Primitive Methodists the Sum of one Hundred, and thirty pounds in full of all principal and Interest due to us as such Trustees, secured on Mortgage of a chapel at New Walsingham the property of the said Trustees. And we hereby undertake at any time when requested by the said Trustees and at their expence to execute such reconveyance of acknowledgment of satisfaction or other document for the purpose of discharging the said Mortgage as may be required for exonerating the said Chapel. therefrom.

Signed —

Franklin Young
William Baker Lane
James Wasey
Edmd Heuau

Trustees

21

(b) Local Preachers

The term Local Preachers dates from the time of Wesley and refers to laymen and women who remain in their own locality and to the present time they continue to be the local preaching strength in Methodism.

A local preacher after training becomes "fully accredited" having gone through the various stages of preparation and training, first "on note" in that a man or woman has been given "a note" to preach. He or she then proceeds to be "on trial" in which he or she is engaged in study and training. When "accredited", the Local Preacher comes on full Plan" that is on the Circuit Preaching Plan each quarter.

Important to the ministry is the quarterly meeting of all Local Preachers in a circuit, which is attended by ordained ministers, in which business is dealt with and when matters of faith and discipline are shared. The minutes of meetings in the Walsingham Wesleyan Circuit in the 19th Century available in the Norwich Record Office provide interesting reading and illustrate the ministry of Local Preachers in the Walsingham Circuit.

Below are examples -
The meeting of 27th December 1843 shows in answering the question,
"Are there any objections to any of the brethren."
that "Bro. "A" having refused to submit himself to the discipline of the Body is hereby suspended for the next three months."

"That Bro."N"s apologies for not attending the meeting be received and that he be required to attend the 2nd March Meeting when the charges against him will be investigated." Such was the discipline within the Local Preachers Meeting.

It is interesting to note that at the Local Preachers Meeting on 27th March 1844, Bro. "N" was present, the charges against him were settled to the satisfaction of the meeting.

In addition, at the same meeting "'HA' having embraced and preached doctrines opposed to the word of God, shall be left off the Plan."

Later in the century, at a meeting on 30th September 1878 in answer to the usual question of any objections to any of the brethren, the Rev. Norman was asked to speak to Bro. "M" with regard to his neglecting his appointments.

Four other brethren were to preach trial sermons for examination at the next Quarterly meeting with a view to going on "full plan".

A move to Congregationalism was anticipated by Bro. "B" in the 3rd October Meeting in 1881.

The meeting of 26th September 1882 reports that "Mr. "W" was not considered satisfactory and it was desired that he should respect-fully be urged to overcome difficulties and by God's help to take a little more work." Details are not given!

At the Local Preachers Meeting on 1st October 1837 we read,

"Bro. "T" to be spoken to by the Superintendent on the subject of returning home after preaching in Hindringham in the afternoon instead of remaining to fulfil his appointment in the evening."

2nd April 1838, "The Superintendent read a note from Bro. Davy regarding his office among us, with a view to uniting himself with the Primitive Methodists. And no doubt was entertained by the meeting of his having done this under the idea of becoming an itinerant preacher among them. This is a circumstance of considerable surprise and regret."

Yet we read in the minutes of the next quarter, 2nd July 1838 - "Bro. Davy …. has returned to his office and duties among us … having resigned them only about four weeks."

This shows that there were occasional switches of allegiance!

On 3rd September 1839 "John Clarke of Old Walsingham have his initials on the plan as an Exorter and a few appointments."
N.B. The designation of Exorter was a preliminary of being placed "on note".

2nd October 1850 Local Preacher Meeting records that the meeting agreed to "Bro. "C" to be spoken to during the next month in order to reform his mind on subjects relating to Methodism and discipline."

In September 1854, the offence of "Neglecting to meet in class ..." is recorded.

These examples show the rigid structure and discipline exercised by the Local Preachers Meeting in the 19th Century. I presume that in the present day, these structures are still in place, but the manner in which they are exercised may have been somewhat modified!

Local Preaching was and still is a great and demanding vocation. A widespread circuit like Walsingham in the 19th Century, would make great demands on its Local Preachers none less than the difficulties of transport. Preachers often had to walk miles to appointments or if fortunate could use the circuit horse!

(c) Sunday Schools

Sunday schools became very much a part of the life of all Methodist Chapels. The 1851 Religious Census showed that the two Methodist Chapels in Walsingham had a total of 90 Sunday School scholars attending on the day of the census.

At first these Sunday schools provided a basic grounding in the 3Rs and children received as much as six or seven hours of teaching in the schools. Although the 1814 Wesleyan Methodist Conference forbade the teaching of writing, and again in 1832 it was evident that the Conference had not the jurisdiction to enforce the rule.

Until the middle of the 19th Century Sunday Schools were concerned largely with secular education, teaching children to read and write which enabled children to gain religious knowledge for themselves. Supporting this is the evidence that "in 1876 the Primitive Methodist Book Rooms issued 17,562 spelling books for their Sunday Schools' use."

For many labourers, attendance at the Methodist Sunday school was all the education they received, as was the case of George Edwards.

Throughout the 19th Century, Sunday school buildings attached to Chapels 'were erected as was the case in Walsingham when the schoolroom was built in 1890. Events such as the Sunday School Anniversary were highlights for the children of the Chapels. The order of service for the Wesleyan Sunday School in Walsingham for Sunday 5th June 1864, now on view in the Chapel, shows children much involved in this event.

In the Fakenham Circuit Report for 1851 for Primitive Methodists, Walsingham was shown as having five male and four female teachers in the Sabbath School as it was called, with 30 male and 55

female pupils, and in the question, "If the circuit is prosperous say in what respect" the minister replies,
"In an increase in -   congregations
                           numbers of events
                           place in Societies
                           Sabbath Schools
                           and Sabbath School children."

1853 shows an increase with 19 teachers and 117 children.

(d) Women's Activities

In the 19th Century, women were active but not prominent in local Wesleyan Methodist circles. In the early days of Methodism, Bebbington notes that "in the proliferating cottage meetings of early Evangelicalism it was often women who took the lead in prayer and praise, counsel and exhortation."

We learn however that the Wesleyans prohibited female preaching for the sake of propriety, however, the custom was restored by the Primitive Methodists. D. W. Bebbington claims that "philanthropy was a major channel for women's energies." A. T. Pierson refers to it as "The Epiphany of Women." This would have included such gatherings at the Sunday School, the Christian Endeavour and Mission Support.

The place of women, even at the end of the 19th Century, among the Walsingham Wesleyans, then part of the Dereham Circuit, showed on the Circuit Plan only two women named among the chapel officers for the whole circuit. In addition, there were no women Local Preachers and only one Leader of Christian Fellow-ship, Miss Watts of Walsingham for Juniors. This is not to say that women were not active in Walsingham Methodism of both tradi-tions. There was a constant demand to raise funds. Extracts from minutes of the quarterly Wesleyan circuit meetings for 1857 read - "It was unanimously agreed that Tea Meetings be held in as many of our places as possible in order if profitable to discharge the circuit debt." And in the meeting of Tuesday 28th March 1865 -

"The Chairman's suggestion that a Ladies Sewing Society be organised with a view to raise the income of the circuit, to be considered, and if possible carried out."

Women played an important part in the domestic activities of the Chapel but not in leadership, particularly among the Wesleyans. Primitive Methodists had already accredited women Local Preachers.

(e) The Quarterly Meetings and the Circuit Schedules

Extracts from other records tell much of the life of the Circuit. The Circuit Schedule Book is of great interest.

It should be noted that a Minute of Conference 1835 Page 118 stated "It is directed that a "Volume of Schedules" be kept in every circuit in which an account of:-
>   the numbers in Society
>   and on trial
>   amount of subscriptions and collections
and other similar records be kept."

Some extracts are revealing:-

Meeting - 28th September 1840
"Resolved that as we have no Society in Hindringham, and Bro. Oughton having left the Chapel there to the "Ranters" for five years, the place be given up for the present, not least during the winter."
N.B. The Chapel referred to is no longer in use, but the Primitive Methodists built a Chapel later in the century.

Meeting - 31st December 1840
"A letter should be addressed by the stewards to the Leaders of each Class .... urging upon them the necessity of raising 2/- per member per quarter in the average, in their respective classes."

Meeting - 27th September 1843
Memo "Mr. Baker undertakes to keep the circuit horse upon condition of the Local Preachers' Board allowing him £2 per quarter."

(f) Pastoral Oversight

Further examples of the ministers' pastoral oversight of his flock are demonstrated in the Station returns of the Fakenham Primitive Methodist Circuit which included Walsingham.

1851 Under "Remarks" the minister writes -
"Dear Brethren, I have assisted 30 families weekly on an average except in the harvest month when the Preachers do not preach in this district." An arrangement obviously to assist with pressures of the harvest.

In 1852 in answer to the question, "What persons who were official character have been separated from the connexion during this year and for what cause?" the reply reads -
"1.   C. W., the cause, stolen goods being found in his house.
2.   J. S. - the cause, fornication.
3.   D. V. - the cause, the person - who is now his wife - being pregnant before marriage."

In 1853 the reply to the same question reads, "cause - familiarised with a young female."

These replies demonstrate the severity of Methodist discipline on matters of morals!

(g) The Class Meeting

What happened in the Class Meetings must have varied from place to place, time to time, and leader to leader, but the leader was normally a layman, that is, he was neither an ordained clergyman nor a Methodist itinerant preacher, - and very often of humble origin or no education, the same applied to the members of his Class for the most part, although it was by no means unknown for an employer to be in the Class led by one of his employees. Prayer at the meeting was certainly extemporaneous and not limited to the leader, the conversation concerned personal matters and included confession of sins as well as testimony to the power of God.

Members absent through sickness or old age were regularly visited by the leader and others, and if necessary, financially supported and those absent for other reasons were pleaded to resume their attendance. Classes for women were separated from those of men and for this reason women Class Leaders played an important part from the start.

Membership of Class and therefore of the Methodist Society required - simply "the desire to flee from the Wrath to come." But those who had experienced the New Birth and were advancing towards Christian Perfection (N.B. in Wesley's mind to be regenerate implied at once the obligation to go on to perfection) -. were gathered in "bands" - smaller groups also led to laymen, in which the higher reaches of the Christian life could be explored. What was said "in band" was held to be completely secret and unrepeatable.

Originally the meeting was partly financial and it became a meeting point "its primary function was a locus in which those who already had the form of godliness might seek the power of it"

It usually consisted of a dozen members meeting weekly in a house or farm building. The Class Leader knew each member well and visited them.

In the records kept, the progress of individuals was shown on the quarterly circuit return. An example can be found in the Quarterly Schedules. For September 1869, Walsingham Wesleyan recorded -

Class Meetings
"Leader - Bro. Woodbine
  - 1 member on trial
  - 2 Emigrations
  - 3 Backsliders
  - 15 now in Society.

Leader - Bro. Watts
  - 1 on trial
  - 1 Emigration
  - 0 Backsliders
  - 13 now in Society.

Old Walsingham
  - 1 Emigration
  - 11 now in society.
Total for Old and New Walsingham 39.

Quarterage received when tickets were rendered.
Public Collection - 15s - 2d.
Worn-out Ministers, and Widows Fund - 5s - 10d."

N.B. At this time, Old Walsingham did not have a Wesleyan Chapel.

Chapter Five

The End of the Century

The end of the 19th Century saw the re-drawing of circuit boundaries with the division of the Walsingham Wesleyan Methodist Circuit. Walsingham became part of the new Dereham Circuit.

The Circuit Book of Quarterly Meetings report a discussion of this:-

3rd July 1887.
"Moved by Mr. Faircloth "That this meeting re-affirms its entire approval for the scheme for the division of the circuit as sanctioned by the District Meeting, and heartily reciprocates the fraternal sentiments of the Dereham brethren."

The Dereham Circuit Plan for the May-August quarter of 1895 gives a very good indication of the life and worship of Wesleyan Methodism in Walsingham at the end of the 19th Century, as seen on the Plan on display in Walsingham Methodist Church. On it we note the announcement of the laying of the Foundation stone of the new Chapel at Old Walsingham on Monday 6th May in the afternoon. The Chairman of the District, the Rev. J. Gould of Cambridge was the speaker. Until this time, Methodists in Old Walsingham had worshipped in a house registered in 1797, but records show that people of Old Walsingham were much associated with the Wesleyan Chapel in Little Walsingham. Of the services, the plan of 1895 shows one service only at Old Walsingham on Sunday afternoons.

Little Walsingham Chapel shows two services on Sundays at 2.00 p.m. and 6.30 p.m., Prayer Meetings on Monday at 7.30 p.m. and a Preaching Service on Wednesdays at 7.30 p.m. The Sunday School Anniversary was designated for 26th May, an event which was important in the life of all the Chapels. Music and recitations by the scholars were special features, as shown by the printed programme displayed in the church today. The traditional new hats and frocks for the girls and knickerbockers and bow ties for the boys as seen in many local photographs show the importance of the Anniversary.

The Chapels had to be self-supporting with additional financial demands for the circuit and the Connexion. The Plan of 1895 show collections at Walsingham on designated Sundays for:-
    Quarterly Collection
    Circuit Aid Collection
    House Missions Collection
    Aged Ministers and Ministers
    Widows' Fund
    District Mission Collection.

In addition, other collections were made throughout the year for the following causes:-
    Horse Hire Fund Collection
    General Chapel Fund
    Wesley Education Fund
    Auxiliary Fund
    New Kingswood and Woodhouse Grove Schools
    Wesleyan Theological Institution.

The spiritual and social need of the members of the chapel are well provided for in addition to the regular weekly services. The plan shows-
    -   Quarterly Love Feast
    -   Sacrament of the Lord's Supper
    -   Camp Meeting (3 are designated for this 1895 quarter)
    -   Covenant Services (First Sunday of the new year)
    -   Chapel Anniversary
    -   Harvest Thanksgiving.

The Plan advertises meetings for Christian Fellowship and Testimony at Walsingham.

Leader	Mr. W Wright
Leader	Mr. G Back
Leader	Mr. W Woodcock
Leader	Miss Watts (Juniors).

The layout of the Plan is similar to that in use today, but several interesting duties indicate the Victorian era and the life of the Chapel.

For example, under the list of circuit officers we read -
"Secretary and Treasurer of the Horse-hire fund - Mr. J. W. Merry"
Obviously indicating the main means of transport for preachers and ministers.

Under notes, we read with reference to the Quarterly Meeting -
"The Society stewards are requested to meet the Circuit stewards at 2.45 o'clock to pay the Quarterage from the several societies."
Thus we see that finance is still important and fundraising essential.

A further notice states "The Chapels of Dereham, Walsingham and Fakenham are only licensed for the Solemnisation of Marriage." The Certificate of 1869 is held in the Fakenham Circuit safe and the Account Book for the Walsingham Chapel records a collection of 11s. by Mr. Stanford towards the registering of the Walsingham Chapel for marriages. The entry is dated 1872 and Kelly's Directory of 1875 records Mr. Stanford of High Street as a Draper and Tailor.

I John Wright — Superintendent Registrar of the District of Walsingham — in the County of Norfolk — do hereby certify, That the Building named The Wesleyan Methodist Chapel — situated at ——— in the Parish of Little Walsingham in the County of Norfolk — having been duly certified as a place of Public Religious Worship, was registered for the Solemnization of Marriage therein, on the twenty seventh day of September — in the Year of our Lord One thousand eight hundred and sixty nine.

Witness my hand, this twenty seventh day of September in the Year of our Lord One thousand eight hundred and sixty nine.

Wright.

Superintendent Registrar.

Licence for the Solemnisation of Marriage

The Plan also states-
"Our Ministers have now the right to officiate at funerals in any churchyard in the country," a right previously denied to Dissenting Ministers "but 48 hours notice must be given to the clergyman on an appropriate form".

Finally at the bottom of the Plan we read-
"Every Methodist family should take a copy of the East Anglian Methodist Church Record - 40 pages of Connexional and Local Information - Price 1d."

Thus we see that the Circuit Plan for 1895 of the Wesleyan Methodist Circuit shows a lively and active Wesleyan Methodist presence in Old and New Walsingham.

Conclusion

Methodism contributed a great deal to the spiritual, social and educational life of the village which reflected the whole situation of 19th Century Great Britain and Ireland.

Methodism was firmly established as a Christian Denomination although divided by the various strands of Methodism. It continued to be a strong spiritual movement of committed Christians which provided the social life of the community and, until 1870 when compulsory education was provided by the state, was an important educational contribution. Life in all its aspects centred round the Chapel which provided a spiritual home and the guardianship of individuals' religious and social freedoms.

Flower arrangement in Walsingham Wesleyan Methodist Church during Ecumenical Festival of Flowers for the Centenary of R.C. Pilgrimage

Bibliography

PRIMARY SOURCES

Detailed references are available from the Author, but a summary is shown here.

Programme displayed in Walsingham Church
Plan displayed in Walsingham Church for 1895.

From County Record Office, Norwich:

Wesleyan Methodism
FC 61/80   Circuit Schedules 1867 - 77
            including correspondence on grant to Walsingham 1869
FC 61/81   Marriage Registers 1869 - 96 for Walsingham and Docking Circuit.
FC 75/32   Stewards Account 1867 - 82 with Quarterly Meeting Minutes.
FC 18/1-14 Variety of documents relating to Circuit and Walsingham Chapel.
FC 18/143   Quarterly Accounts 1834 - 67.
FC 18/144   Chapel Census return 1881.

Primitive Methodism
FC 18/17-93
FC 18/17 -24 Quarterly Meetings and Local Preachers' Meeting Minutes.
FC 18/52-66 Circuit Reports and Chapel Schedules 1847 - 1882
FC 18/67-93 Roll Books 1899 onwards.
Circuit Archives - Fakenham. Deeds, Trustees, Certificates.

SECONDARY SOURCES

Arch, J.   "The Story of his Life."
                    1898 - Hutchinson, London.
Barton, David A.   "Discovering Chapels and Meeting Houses."
                    1990 - Shire Publications Ltd.
Bebbington, D. W.   "Evangelisation in Modern Britain."
                    1993 - Routledge, London.
Bewes, Richard   "John Wesley's England."
                    1981 - The Seabury Press, New York.
Brew, F. E.   "The English Agricultural Labourer."
                    1920 - P.S. King.
Chadwick, Owen   "The Victorian Church, Part I 1829 - 1859,
                    Part II 1860 - 1901."
                    1971 - S.C.M. Press, London.
Davies, Ruport E.   "Methodism."
                    1985 - Epworth Press, Westminster.

Edwards, George "From Crow-scaring to Westminster - An Autobiography."
1922 - Labour Publishing Co.
Evans, Eric J. "The Forging of the Modern State 1783 - 1870."
1996 - Longman, London and New York.
Henshaw, J. "The Romance of the Sunday School".
1910 - London.
Jolly, Cyril "The Spreading Flame - the coming of Methodism to Norfolk."
(No date given) Published privately by Cyril Jolly, Dereham.
Leary, William and "A Methodist Guide to Lincolnshire and East Anglia."
Vickers, John. 1984. World Methodist Historical Soc. Publication.
(British Section).
Moore, James (Ed) "Religion in Victorian Britain." III sources.
1988 - O.U. in association with
Manchester University Press.
Pierson, A. T. Forward Movements of the Last Half Century."
1900 - New York.
Royle, Edward "Modern Britain - a social History 1750 - 1995."
1957 - Arnold, London and New York.
Scotland, Nigel "Methodism and the Revolt of the Field."
1981 - Alan Sutton, Gloucester.
Springall, L. Marion. "Labourly Life in Norfolk Village 1834 - 1914".
1936 - Allen & Unwin.
Tabraham, Barrie W. "The Making of Methodism."
1995 - Epworth Press, Westminster.
Wade-Martin, P. (Ed) "An Historical Atlas of Norfolk."
1993 - Norfolk Museum Service.

ALSO

"The Primitive
Methodist Magazine" A selection of extracts, 1843, 1813.
Christmas, J. F. 1993. Street Map, 19th Century Little Walsingham.
Kelly & Co. Post Office Directory. 1830, 1836, 1845, 1854, 1864, 1875,
1879, 1900.
Kelly & Co. Publishing Office, London.
Haigh, Rev. J. "Little Walsingham Methodist Church."
1996 Pamphlet for Visitors.
Stevens, Rev. J. and "Methodism through the Ages."
Beaumont, J. Circuit circulation.
Archaeological Society, Plan of Friary from "The Greyfriars of Walsingham."
Martin, A. R. 1933 - Norwich.

APPENDICES:

A List of the Members in Society in the Walsingham Circuit - 1802.

William Wedrill - Farmer
Lewis Minn - Miller
John Minn - Baker
Henry Bircham - Tanner
Roger Barns - Labourer
Samuel Andrews - Labourer
Mary Andrew
Tom Priest - Labourer
Jane Priest
Hannah Kinstead
Thos. Rumbles - Labourer
Alice Bond
John Bircham - Labourer
Wm Palmer - Carpenter
Fanny Wilshaw
Frances Wilshaw
Mary Lown
Sarah Olly
Ann Blofield
Amy Baldwin
Wm Livley - Carpenter
Wm Lambert - Baker
Thos. Curzon - Shoe-maker
Margaret Curb
Peter Thurgood - Pattern Maker
Elizabeth Wedrill
Sarah Minns
Ann Curzon
Thos. Bond -
Mary Minn
Mary Wilshire
Elizabeth Lambert
1 local Preacher
8 New Members
31 in society

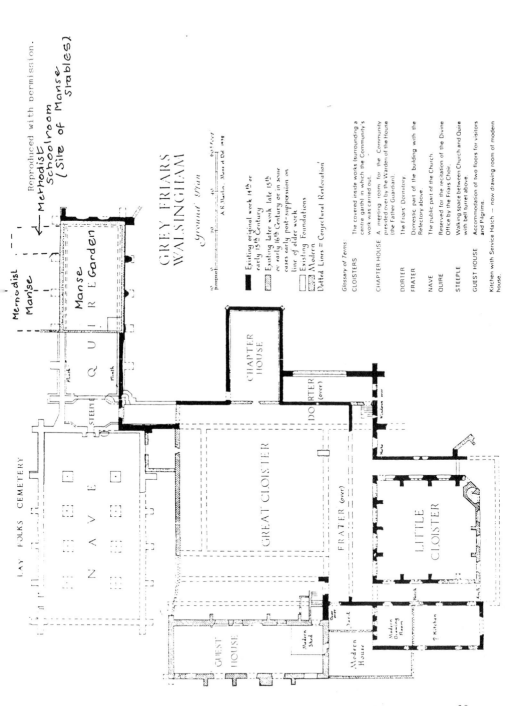

GREY FRIARS
WALSINGHAM

Ground Plan

A.R. Wells March Oct 1938

■ Existing original work 14th or early 15th Century

▨ Existing later work late 15th or early 16th Century or in some cases early post-suppression on line of older work

□ Existing Foundations
□ Modern
Dotted Lines = Conjectural Restoration

Glossary of Terms:

CLOISTERS — The covered inside works (surrounding a centre garth) in which the Community's work was carried out.

CHAPTER HOUSE — A meeting room for the Community presided over by the Warden of the House (the Father Guardian).

DORTER — The Friars' Dormitory

FRATER — Domestic part of the building with the Refectory above

NAVE — The public part of the Church

QUIRE — Reserved for the recitation of the Divine Office by the Friars Choir.

STEEPLE — Walking space between Church and Quire with bell turret above.

GUEST HOUSE — Accommodation of two floors for visitors and Pilgrims.

Kitchen with Service Hatch — now drawing room of modern house.

Reproduced with permission.

Methodist Schoolroom (Site of Manse Stables)

Methodist Manse

Manse

QUIRE Garden

STEEPLE

CHAPTER HOUSE

DORTER (over)

LAY FOLKS CEMETERY

NAVE

GREAT CLOISTER

FRATER (over)

LITTLE CLOISTER

GUEST HOUSE

Modern House

Modern Shed

Modern Drawing Room

Kitchen

39

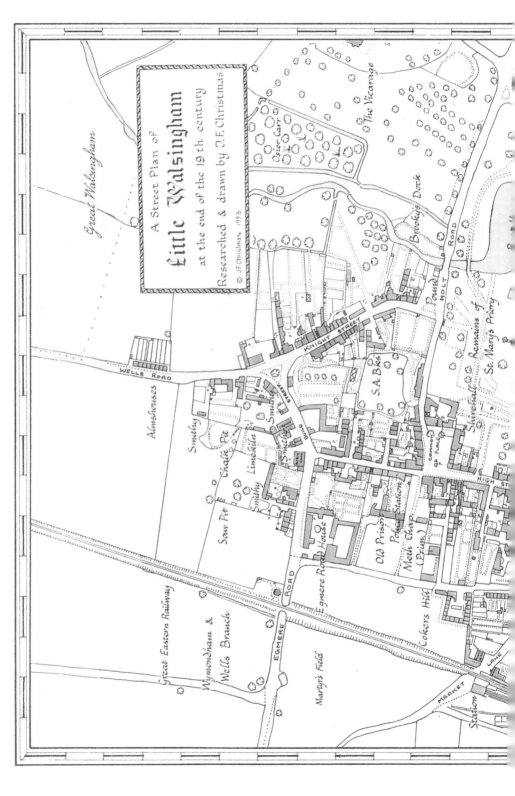

A Street Plan of

Little Walsingham

at the end of the 19th century

Researched & drawn by J.F.Christmas

© J.F.Christmas 1993

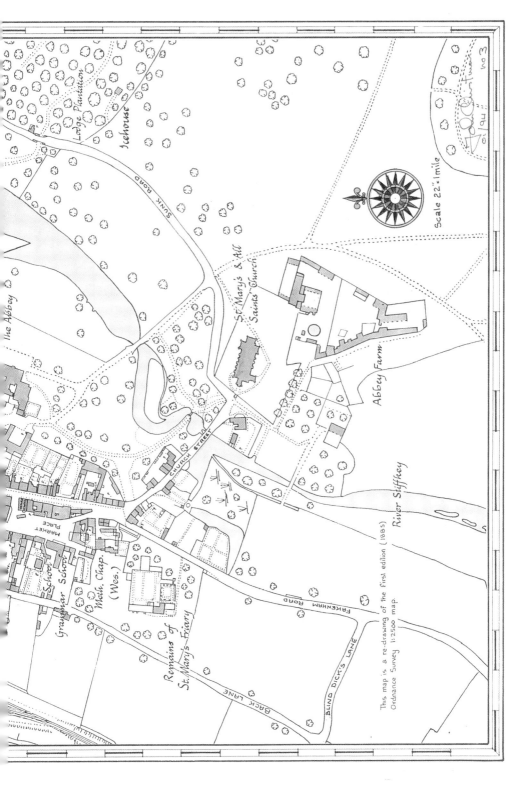

No 3

Scale 22" = 1 mile

Lodge Plantation

Icehouse

SUNK ROAD

The Abbey

St Mary's & All Saints Church

Abbey Farm

River Stiffkey

CHURCH STREET

MARKET PLACE

School

Grammar School

Weth. Chap. (Wes.)

Remains of St Mary's Friary

FAKENHAM ROAD

BLIND DICK'S LANE

BACK LANE

This map is a re-drawing of the first edition (1885) Ordnance Survey 1:2500 map.

Census of Great Britain, 1851.

(13 and 14 Victoria, cap. 53).

A RETURN

OF THE SEVERAL PARTICULARS TO BE INQUIRED INTO RESPECTING THE UNDERMENTIONED

PLACE OF PUBLIC RELIGIOUS WORSHIP.

[N.B.—A similar Return will be obtained from the Clergy of the Church of England, and also from the Minister of every other Religious Denomination throughout Great Britain.]

I. Name or Title of Place of Worship	II. Where Situate; specifying the			III. Religious Denomination	IV. When Erected	V. Whether a Separate and Entire Building	VI. Whether used exclusively as a Place of Worship (Except for a Sunday School)	VII. Space available for Public Worship		VIII. Estimated Number of Persons attending Divine Service on Sunday, March 30, 1851			IX. REMARKS
	Parish, or Place (1)	District (2)	County (3)					Number of Sitting already Provided (4) Free Sittings / Other Sittings	Free Space or Standing Room for	Morning	Afternoon	Evening	
Wesleyan Chapel	Walsingham	Walsingham	Norfolk	Wesleyan Methodists	Before 1800	Yes	Yes	220 220		General Congregation — 146 70		— 146 70	
										Sunday Scholars — ½	—	—	
										TOTAL 17 146 70			
										Average Number of Attendants during months (See Instruction VIII) General Congregation — 200 80			
										Sunday Scholars — ½	—	—	
										TOTAL ..			

I certify the foregoing to be a true and correct Return to the best of my belief. Witness my hand this 31st day of March 1851.

X. (Signature) ...... Ministry for ____ of the above-named Place of Worship

(Official Character) Minister for Sixty

(Address by Post) Walsingham

Norfolk

The particulars to be inserted in Divisions I. to VI. inclusive, and in IX., may be written either along or across the columns, as may be more convenient.

Census of Great Britain, 1851.

(13 and 14 Victoria, cap. 53).

A RETURN

OF THE SEVERAL PARTICULARS TO BE INQUIRED INTO RESPECTING THE UNDERMENTIONED

PLACE OF PUBLIC RELIGIOUS WORSHIP.

[N. B.—A similar Return will be required from the Clergy of the Church of England, and also from the Ministers of every other Religious Denomination throughout Great Britain]

I.	II.			III.	IV.	V.	VI.	VII.		VIII.				IX.
Name or Title of Place of Worship	Where Situate; specifying the			Religious Denomination	When Erected	Whether a Separate and Entire Building	Whether used exclusively as a Place of Worship (Except for a Sunday School)	Space available for Public Worship. Number of Sittings already Provided		Estimated Number of Persons attending Divine Service on Sunday, March 30, 1851				REMARKS
	Parish or Place (1)	District (2)	County (3)					Free Sittings (1)	Other Sittings (2)		Morning	Afternoon	Evening	
Wes..	Walsingham	Walsingham	Norfolk	Wesleyan		No	No	180	150	General Congregation / Sunday Scholars / TOTAL..	34	X	X	
								Free Space or Standing Room for		Average Number of Attendants during 12 months (See Instruction VIII.) General Congregation / Sunday Scholars / TOTAL ..				

I certify the foregoing to be a true and correct Return to the best of my belief. Witness my hand this 31 day of _March_ 1851.

x (Signature) ...... _Robert Freeman_

(Official Character) _Local Preacher_ of the above-named Place of Worship

(Address by Post) _Robert Freeman of Walsingham_
Norfolk

The particulars to be inserted in Divisions I. to VI. inclusive, and in IX., may be written either along or across the columns, as may be more convenient.

43

Census of Great Britain, 1851.

(13 and 14 Victoriæ, cap. 53).

A RETURN

OF THE SEVERAL PARTICULARS TO BE INQUIRED INTO RESPECTING THE UNDERMENTIONED

PLACE OF PUBLIC RELIGIOUS WORSHIP.

[N.B.—A similar Return will be obtained from the Clergy of the Church of England, and also from the Ministers of every other Religious Denomination throughout Great Britain]

I.	II.			III.	IV.	V.	VI.	VII.			VIII.				IX.
Name or Title of Place of Worship	Where Situate; specifying the			Religious Denomination	When Erected	Whether a Separate and Entire Building	Whether used exclusively as a Place of Worship (Except for a Sunday School)	Space available for Public Worship			Estimated Number of Persons attending Divine Service on Sunday, March 30, 1851				REMARKS
	Parish or Place (1)	District (2)	County (3)					Number of Sittings already Provided		Free Space or Standing Room for		Morning	Afternoon	Evening	
								Free Sittings (1)	Other Sittings (2)						
Primitive Methodist Chapel.	Walsingham	Norwich.	Norfolk.	Primitive Methodist Connexion	1848	Yes	Yes	50	146	None, except the ___	General Congregation	73	142	142	
											Sunday Scholars				
											Total...	73	142	142	
											Average Number of Attendants during months (See Instruction VIII)				
											General Congregation				
											Sunday Scholars				
											TOTAL...				

I certify the foregoing to be a true and correct Return to the best of my belief.

Witness my hand this 20" day of March 1851

X (Signature) ...... William Ward

(Official Character) Primitive Methodist Minister

(Address by Post) Near Walsingham

Norfolk

The particulars to be inserted in Divisions I. to VI. inclusive, and in IX., may be written either along or across the columns, as may be more convenient.

Census of Great Britain, 1851.

(13 and 14 Victoriæ, cap. 53).

A RETURN

OF THE SEVERAL PARTICULARS TO BE INQUIRED INTO RESPECTING THE UNDERMENTIONED

PLACE OF PUBLIC RELIGIOUS WORSHIP.

[N.B.—A similar Return will be obtained from the Clergy of the Church of England, and also from the Minister of every other Religious Denomination throughout Great Britain.]

I. Name or Title of Place of Worship	II. Where Situate; specifying the			III. Religious Denomination	IV. When Erected	V. Whether a Separate and Entire Building	VI. Whether used exclusively as a Place of Worship (Except for a Sunday School)	VII. Space available for Public Worship		VIII. Estimated Number of Persons attending Divine Service on Sunday, March 30, 1851			IX. REMARKS
	Parish or Place (1)	District (2)	County (3)					Number of Sittings already Provided		Morning	Afternoon	Evening	
Independent Chapel	Walsingham		County of Norfolk	Independent	1810	Separate & Entire	Used exclusively as a place of worship.	Free Sittings (1) 40	Other Sittings (2) 110	4000	160 7	—	
								Free Space or Standing Room for		General Congregation Sunday Scholars Total...			
										Average Number of Attendants during months (See Instruction VIII.) General Congregation Sunday Scholars Total...	58	69	

I certify the foregoing to be a true and correct Return to the best of my belief.

Witness my hand this Thirtieth day of March 1851.

x (Signature) ...... John Summers

(Official Character) Minister

(Address by Post) John Summers Walsingham Norfolk

The particulars to be inserted in Divisions I. to VI. inclusive, and in IX., may be written either along or across the columns, as may be more convenient.

Census of Great Britain, 1851.

(13 and 14 Victoria; cap. 53).

A RETURN

OF THE SEVERAL PARTICULARS TO BE INQUIRED INTO RESPECTING THE UNDERMENTIONED

PLACE OF PUBLIC RELIGIOUS WORSHIP.

[N.B.—A *similar Return will be obtained from the Clergy of the Church of England, and also from the Ministers of every other Religious Denomination throughout Great Britain*.]

I. Name or Title of Place of Worship	II. Where Situate; specifying the Parish or Place (1)	District (2)	County (3)	III. Religious Denomination	IV. When Erected	V. Whether a Separate and Entire Building	VI. Whether used exclusively as a Place of Worship (Except for a Sunday School)	VII. Space available for Public Worship — Number of Sittings already Provided: Free Sittings (1) / Other Sittings (2)	Free Space or Standing Room for	VIII. Estimated Number of Persons attending Divine Service on Sunday, March 30, 1851 — Morning / Afternoon / Evening	Average Number of Attendants during three months (See Instruction VIII.)	IX. REMARKS
										General Congregation — x / 64 / 60		
										Sunday Scholars — / 64 / 60		
										Total...		
									50	General Congregation — x / 50 / 50		
										Sunday Scholars — / 50 / 60		
										Total...		

I certify the foregoing (to be a true and correct Return to the best of my belief.

Witness my hand this 31st day of March 1851.

x (Signature) ...... Joseph Curton

(Official Character) Manager

(Address by Post) J. Curton

...... of the above-named Place of

The particulars to be inserted in Divisions I. to VI. inclusive, and in IX., may be written either along or across the columns, as may be more convenient.

A SHORT ACCOUNT OF
WESLEYANISM IN THE COUNTY OF NORFOLK
ESPECIALLY IN
THE WALSINGHAM CIRCUIT

This County was early favoured with the self-denied and fruitful labours of the great and good Wesleys, and their devoted Preachers. The Wesleys first visited the City of Norwich in 1754; but in 1749 Norwich stood on the first list of Circuits. In 1765, two preachers are named, and two years later we find 293 members. In 1776, Lynn became a circuit town, and in the county there were 6 Preachers and 645 members. In 1791, the year the great Wesley passed to heaven, we find our circuits, Wells being one, 10 Preachers and 1260 Members; 1811, 6 circuits, 18 Preachers and 3517 Members; 1880, 19 circuits, 39 Preachers and 6401 Members.

October, 1781, Mr. Wesley visited Walsingham, Wells and Fakenham, as we read in his Journals. Walsingham became a circuit town in 1792, with 2 Ministers and about 200 members. After the lapse of 88 years, and the transfer of societies to other circuits, there were 311 Members in 16 places, including 14 Chapels, 2 Ministers, 25 Local Preachers, and 9 on trial. May the Lord speedily and abundantly revive his work. The following list of Ministers who have travelled in the circuit may gratify many.-

1792	William Denton, Henry Anderson
1793	William Denton, Isaac Lilly
1794	William Heath, Francis West
1795	William Heath, John Witham
1796	John Sanderson, Josiah Hill
1797	Benjamin Leggatt, Charles Martin
1798	Benjamin Leggatt, Francis Collier
1799	Robert Hardacre, Thomas Dunn
1800	Robert Hardacre, John Cricket
1801-2	Edward Gibbons, John Wilshaw
1803-4	Caleb Simmons, William Breedon
1805	Marmaduke Revell, James Burley
1806	Marmaduke Revell, John Julian
1807	William Gilpin, John Bumstead
1808	William Gilpin, John King
1809	John Newton, Francis Burgess
1810	John Newton, Thomas Stringer, Corbett Cooke
1811	James Penman, William Hinson, Thomas Davies
1812	James Penman, William Hinson, Thomas Rolfe
1813	Josiah H Walker, George Moorhouse, Richard Shepherd
1814	Thomas Slugg, Moses Dunn, Joseph Hutton
1815	Thomas Slugg, Joseph Hutton
1816-17	George Douglas, William Bacon
1818	Arthur Hutchinson, Archbld Mc. Laughlin
1819	Arthur Hutchinson, Thomas Morgan
1820-21	Ebenezer Stewart, James Jones, jnr
1822	William Breedon, Matthew Mallinson
1823	William Breedon, Jarvis Shaw
1824-26	Robert Byrant, Thomas Catterick
1827	Edward Chapman, John Smithson
1828	Edward Chapman, Jonathan J. Bates
1829	Robert Morton, Jonathan J. Bates
1830	Robert Morton, John W. Barritt
1831	James Bate, John W. Barritt
1832-33	James Bate, Geoge North
1834	Humphery Stephenson, James Lancaster, Joseph Jackson, junr

1835	Humphery Stephenson, James Lancaster, William Jackson, junr
1836	Thomas Ballinghall, James Pilley, Samuel Hooley
1837	Thomas Ballinghall, Moses Rayner
1838	Moses Rayner, William Hill, junr
1839	Moses Rayner, Charles S. B. Taylor
1840	William Wilson, John Booth
1841-42	Henry Cheverton, Thomas R. Jones
1843	Henry Cheverton, William Baker junr
1844-45	John W. Cotton, William Baker junr
1846-47	John Coates, John Tucker
1848	John Coates, William Baddeley
1849	Richard Tabraham, William Baddeley
1850	Daniel Hateley, William Baddeley
1851	John Mann, Charles B. Richie
1852	James Scott, Charles B. Richie
1853	John Bissell, John Danks
1854	John Bissell
1855-56	Benjamin G. Mitchell
1857-58	William Robinson
1859	Uriah Butters
1860-62	Thomas Pearson (3)
1863-65	William Willey
1866-67	James Cooper
1868	Thompson Hesk, George Sanderson
1869	Thomas Burrows, John Leathley
1870	Thomas Burrows, Stephen G. Scott
1871	John Tesseyman, George Woodcock
1872	George Clement, Samuel Simpson
1873	Christopher B. Sykes, William Ellis
1874	Christopher B. Sykes, John Woollerton
1875	George Meadows, John Woollerton
1876	George Meadows, Caleb Streat
1877	George Meadows, William Morgan
1878	Daniel Eyre, Samuel Norman
1879	Daniel Eyre, S. T. A. De La Mare
1880	Daniel Eyre, Frederick J. Murrell

PRICE THREE PENCE

47

Acknowledgements

To:

- Mr. Howard Fears, MA, for his support and his helpful material.
- The Norfolk Record Office for help in the research and permission to reproduce material.
- The Rev. Malcolm Braddy, MA, Chairman of the Methodist Church, East Anglia District.
- Ms. Pauline West, the District Archivist of the Methodist Church.
- The Open University for material used in Course A.425.
- Mrs. Debbie Parker for assistance in typing and printing.
- Mr. and Mrs. A. Negus for material on Zacharias Walker.
- The Clergy and Circuit Stewards of the Fakenham, Wells and Holt circuit of the Methodist Church for making available historic material.
- Mr. Tom Coleman for photographs.
- The Chapel Steward of Walsingham Methodist Church.
- Members of the village community for assistance with historical material.
- The Walsingham Museum Staff.
- Mrs. H. J. Jolly for her generous gift of "The Spreading Flame", written by her husband, the late Cyril Jolly.
- The Rev John Denny ARIBA for permission to reproduce his drawing of the Priory.
- Mr. John Christmas for permission to reproduce his 19th century street map of Walsingham.

We apologise for any acknowledgements we may have inadvertently overlooked.

The use of the words "Chapel" and "Church" are retained as originally used.